(excerpt from "Journey" pg. 86)

I am now looking through new eyes.
I am now walking through a new world.
I'm starting to blend into this other me.
I have no control over this entity.
I'm simply an undercover observer.

~ **Candice James**

Also by Candice James

10 PAK - 1
A Potpourri of Paintings
The Still Small Voice of Soul
Spiritual Whispers
Atmospheres
Blue Silence
Call of the Crow
Imagination's Reverie
Short Shots 2
The Depth of the Dance
Behind the One-Way Mirror
The Path of Loneliness
Rithimus Aeternam
The Water Poems
Short Shots
City of Dreams
Merging Dimensions
The 13th Cusp
Colors of India
Purple Haze
A Silence of Echoes
Shorelines
Ekphrasticism
Midnight Embers
Bridges and Clouds
Inner Heart, a Journey
A Split in the Water

10 PAK — 2

THE LONG POEMS

by
Candice James

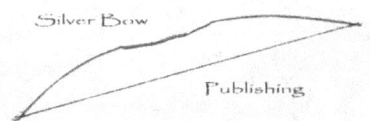

Box 5 - 720 - 6th Street,
New Westminster, BC
V3C 3C5   CANADA

10 PAK — 2 Candice James

Title: 10 PAK -2 The Long Poems
Author: Candice James
Copyright © 2025 Silver Bow Publishing
Cover Painting: "Arctic Ice Flow 1"
  painting by Candice James
Layout/Design: Candice James
ISBN: 9781774033470 (print)
ISBN: 9781774033487 (ebk)j

All rights reserved including the right to reproduce or translate this book or any portions thereof, in any form except for the use of short passages for review purposes, no part of this book may be reproduced, in part or in whole, or transmitted in any form or by any means, electronically or mechanically, including photocopying, recording, or any information or storage retrieval system without prior permission in writing from the publisher or a license from the Canadian Copyright Collective Agency (Access Copyright)
© Silver Bow Publishing 2025

Library and Archives Canada Cataloguing in Publication

Title: 10 PAK-2 : the long poems / by Candice James.
Other titles: Ten PAK-two
Names: James, Candice, 1948- author
Identifiers: Canadiana (print) 20250171988 | Canadiana (ebook) 20250172003 | ISBN 9781774033470
  (softcover) | ISBN 9781774033487 (Kindle)
Subjects: LCGFT: Poetry.
Classification: LCC PS8569.A429 A6123 2025 | DDC C811/.54—dc23

FOREWORD

The poems in this book are long poems set out in such a way as to allow the reader to rest on each page to fully digest the meaning and let their imagination run free to see the visuals and images the words are painting.

This layout gives the reader the best of experiences as they go through the poems and pages.

10 PAK — 2   Candice James

CONTENTS

The Other Side Of The Blue Mirror / 9

The Eyes Of The Dead / 23

This Imaginary House / 33

Leaving / 47

Once Again I Am Waiting / 67

Journey / 81

In The Light / 99

Wings To Fly / 119

A Child Of God / 131

Life And Death / 159

Author Profile / 168

10 PAK – 2   Candice James

The Other Side Of The Blue Mirror

10 PAK — 2   Candice James

I

There is a palpability
to these invisible pluralities
wandering the overgrown pathways
and derelict signposts in my mind.

I am the moving singularity
that carries them from room to room
staring into mirror upon mirror
at the images that are me,

>   or them,
>   or no-one ...

perhaps a doppelganger skulking,
an intruder invading my silence
striking artificial snare drums
causing my teeth to quake
inside this hologram I live in.

Clouds, burnt out stars
and retrograde nightmares abound
in this forsaken dark place
where hazy dreams go to die;
but instead become
stillborn memories.

II

I've searched for diamonds and pearls
in the damp, dusty coal mines of love
and I have bet on the underdog
hoping to beat the odds
throwing caution to the wind
in a topsy-turvy game of never win.

I have turned myself inside out,
gone from green to yellow,
red to purple and finally ended up
back inside the pool
of blue mirrors and tears
I once shed and discarded.

I thought they were dead things,
discarded nothings that had no life;
but they will not stay still.
They haunt me day and night
and I am turning into one of them.

I am becoming a burning tear
trapped in the frigid essence
of a relentless icy blue mirror,
reflecting the fading essence
of the dying ghost I am.

An apparition out of time and space,
I take breath from the atmosphere
I surreptitiously move through
where there is always the hint
of a perpetually renewing star
waiting to be reborn, and born again
to shine on me with pride and disgust,
to light my way out of this doom
I am so unwaveringly trapped in.

This Tsunami that carried me away
did not wander far from me.

Sometimes late at night
inside the cloyed minutes
of trapped midnight hours
I can hear it swishing and sloshing
forming unknown words,
whispering slurs and threats;
but they are blurry and indecipherable.

It may as well be talking to the sun;
but even the sun has gone into hiding
afraid to be caught unaware
in its impending perilous path
when the sleeping tsunami awakens
with a hunger only destruction can sate.

Here it comes and I can't outrun it
so I lay down in its path
that I might withstand its force
and be safely swept into
the ever-present breath
of God's essence.

III

On this side of the blue mirror,
I awaken inside a silken slice of peace;
this is not what I expected at all.

I am inside looking out from
deep inside the blue mirror I am;
and I am outside looking in.
on the other side of the blue mirror.

It's like stepping into another dimension
and swimming in a cosmic pool
where there's no ebbing or ascension.
Just a welcoming warm and vibrant cool.

    Inside the essence of the haze
      everything is crystal clear.
    Life's hours pass by in minutes
inside the second hand of a clock
          in, this,
  the third hand of time's maze.

IV

On the other side of the blue mirror
a beautiful shimmering angel
alights at my side,
and beckons me
to step into the fold of its wings

and ride

the all-knowing static tide of time
that leads to heaven's sea.

As I move in and through the blue
      of the blue mirror I am
I reflect in a million shimmering shades
      and tones of its colours
   that sway and dance and pirouette
      and then turn back into
the full effulgence of the blue mirror.

   The mirror warms me to the bone.
I shed my flesh to walk with the angels:

      No more a singularity.
      Nevermore to be alone.

The Eyes
Of
The Dead

Sometimes at night
when I'm falling asleep
the dead come to my door.

I feel like I'm looking at myself
through the eyes of the dead.

I see myself in the distance
searching for a key I can't find
buried in a burnt-out parking lot
      steeped in ashes
      and twisted metal.

Sometimes at night
when I'm falling asleep
and the dead enter my being,
I see myself in a hospital
wandering the hallways,
looking for elevators or stairways,
searching for exits
that cannot be found.

10 PAK — 2   Candice James

I see myself as someone else.
Someone I know not;
but know very well indeed.

I look into the blurred mirror
and see that someone is me:
       before,
            after,
                 and now.

The dead knock on my door
with the sordid tales
and dreams of a princess
dressed in the tatters of a pauper.

They call her by my name.

They whisper and hide,
inside musty hidden crevices,
in my mausoleum of madness
and shattered beings.

10 PAK — 2   Candice James

These are the auspices
of graven images
and memories buried deep
in the inner recesses of a hazy,
far and away existence
creeping closer each day.

Sometimes at night
when I'm falling asleep

I see myself standing regal and high
on a glistening sacred mountain.

And other times I am crawling
through the mire and misery
of a mud-covered trail.

This is like a pre-amble soliloquy
to setup a movie or book;
        but it isn't.

It's the alleyway into myself,
    into my past lifetimes
        or
a preview of those to come.

I can almost visualize them
  as I look deeper into
     and through
the glazed eyes of the dead.

Sometimes at night
when I'm falling asleep
I feel like I'm looking at myself
through the eyes of the dead.

This Imaginary House

10 PAK — 2   Candice James

This imaginary house I've built,
full of vintage mysticism
and metaphysical paradoxes,
never lacks a heartbeat
or a resonance of soul.

Yesterday's words, colors,
emotions and paintings
still live and breathe
in short gasping inhalations
and long laborious exhalations;
equally seasoned with
spoonfuls of salt
and pinches of pepper
to a flavor balance of perfection.

The road I travel
is a fortress filled with mystery
waiting to be dissected
and then resurrected.
Waiting to be created and probed
then solved and dissolved.

We are the haphazard collection
of all our previous histories.
Mazes to be conquered
or prisons to be trapped in.

We are made of such mysteries.

Magnificence and malaise
in eternal reoccurrence

We make decisions daily:
Do we ride a roller coaster?
Or relax on a carousel horse.
Do we sit in the stands?
Or take part in the race.

When I try to figure out
how the story I am ends
I am always taken back
to the beginning of the end;
an end that continuously
intertwines and circles back
in its never-ending dance
    of life and death and
the irredeemable in-between.

On a bright moonlit day
I saw myself under a blustery sun
tanning and burning simultaneously.
as I laid in cognitive dissonance
beside an ever-changing lavender lake.

Alone, but not lonely, I was at peace
inside a shaker of absolute silence.
I fell into a surreal sleep
inside the back pocket of the lake.

In my lucid dream state
I witnessed the waters of the lake
turn into burning tears
forming a swirling sword
thrust into the artifice of a living stone;
and then I heard the waters whisper
over and over and over again
in a soft harmony of echoes ...

*"Remember your other selves.
Those living, dead and undead.
Remember ... Remember."*

I fell into a deep comforting sleep.
The lake enveloped me in its dream
and revealed eternity's secrets to me.

I began to remember my other selves.

Each hazy figure shuffled by
at a fast, yet slow, pace.
The highlights and lowlights
of their temporary existences
were cast in swirling, succession
then spilled and poured out
like finely aged whiskey
changing into technicolor sequins
forming the cinematic movie
they were, they are
and they will be.

The lake then produced
an ancient amber whiskey barrel
with a gleaming crystal shot glass
resting on top of the unopened barrel;
and the lake whispered,
huskily, through wanton lips:

"Drink, and remember your sins.
Drink, to wash your spirit clean.
Remember, and be reborn again
with the invisibly imprinted knowledge
of the imperfections you must perfect."

I awoke after the deep, long sleep
I remembered the words of the lake
and the lessons and knowledge
imparted to me in echoing silence;
and true enlightenment
filled my being to the brim.

Random thoughts began to imprint
indelible words in my mind:
'The Holographic Universe'.
'Einstein's Monster'
and *'Gravity's Engines'.*

Then I remembered the book;
the book the lake whispered of.

It became my life's quest to find it:
'The Width of a Dwarfed Black Hole'
written in ancient, petrified stone
by an outlaw, renegade star-master.

Thus began my search
in the 5th Dimension of White Holes.

The lake didn't give directions
but I trust in the confidence
of all my selves and spirit
that I will find it in this incarnation:

Enfolded and unfolded.
In between the in between.

10 PAK — 2   Candice James

Leaving

10 PAK — 2   Candice James

10 PAK — 2   Candice James

This imaginary house I've built,
full of vintage mysticism,
and metaphysical paradoxes
never lacks a heartbeat
or a sentience of soul(s).

I

Outside

the lights are dull and hazy
like a lazy dawn yawning
and awakening the sea.
    Skulking
        over it,
    under it,
searching
for something *lost*.

These lights will never gleam,
        never shine again.

Inside

legs and arms
resurrect dead voices
hidden inside forgotten promises,
broken deeds and unsigned covenants.

       BUT

These voices will never be heard.

Above

wingless angels fly,
suspended by frayed strings,
puppets of a demi-god
that is not a god at all.

And yet,
they harken to his call
and continue to flap
their sparse wings.

These broken angels
will never truly soar,
never truly fly.

Below

Hands and feet without shape
become nondescript torn canvasses
and surreal concrete abstractions:
colorless to the point of invisibility
grasping for something ... *lost*.

These appendages are faltering.
Soon they will move no more.

Here

the devil in miniature
adds raw need to each bite
of forbidden fruit savoured.

Inside this anachronistic dream
in the lost and found,
the lost are found
and the found are lost
in the damp, cloyed clutch
and chaotic circumstance
of this human crush ...
        called life.

II

I awaken into a new reality
that is not reality at all;
and yet there is an unsettling
familiarity abounding within.

My memories are like that of
a newborn babe in a strange desert;
but I can still recall the feeling of wet.

I remember this rain:
The texture of its touch.
The timbre of its voice.

The rain speaks in soft staccato
    to the evergreens.
It whispers to the gleaming,
graffiti-carved park benches
    coming forth
from the back-channel recesses
  of a half-lived existence.

 An overcast ghost
chases fading clouds
across a darkening sky;
   and somewhere,
there is a distant beach
trying to catch up with
a summer too far away.

Here, the rain speaks
in many languages and tongues.
In a loud, raspy voice sometimes.
In soft, gentle whispers other times.

And then it stops.

But its lips keep moving,
mouthing secrets and assignations
to desperate lovers living inside
its dangerous climate of moods,
hiding in their own private lies;
desperate lovers like me.

But always, always
>	I remember the rain:

*The texture of its touch;
and the timbre of its voice.*

*When I am dead
remember me ...
remembering the rain.*

III

I will be gone
when you wake tomorrow,
but I do not leave you
empty handed.

To you, my lover, I leave:

My thoughts
to mingle with your daydreams
so you may resist the reality
that I have really gone.

My words
to echo in your castigated ears
that grew conveniently deaf
as I spoke of my truths.

My stone-cold silence
to your icy lips
that so casually bruised my heart.

My second sight
to your fragile artistic fingers
that they may try to paint
the love I offered you.

And finally,
my four bank accounts
with nothing in them
that you may empty them
when you are in need.

To others:

I leave my misdirected passion
to the broken-hearted
still searching for a Nirvana
that can't be found.

To the ragamuffins and beggars
in the streets,
I leave wishes owed to me
that I failed to collect.

To my many disposable friends,
cut-out doll kings and queens,
I leave the meaningless ambitions
and fleeting fame I found
lying beside a graffiti-scarred dumpster
        in a blind alley
alive with a million lacklustre eyes.

To everyone:

I will be gone when you wake tomorrow;
   but I do not leave empty hearted.

No I do not leave empty hearted,

>   I was...
> a poet!

Once Again
I Am Waiting

10 PAK — 2   Candice James

When my chastened heart
yearns for the long- ago,
after before the before,
transient thoughts trip and untangle
invading my calm like a wild wind —
cold, uninvited and unwelcome,
yet calm and warmly soothing.

The yin and yang of living
and the difference between
just living and ... living well.

As I walk the shorelines of eternity
a wandering melancholy evanesces
like a setting moon swallowed whole
in the waves of a tsunami ocean,

There is no buoyancy here,
on this wet, faux asphalt highway
of viscosity and governed velocity,
only undercurrents and whirlpools
and churned-up renegade riptides
announcing the untimely death
of a love too hot not to burn out.

Long after the body bliss,
laying in the arms of limitless love,
the reborn spirit seeks communion
and is given blessed redemption.

I hang in the balance quivering
in an heavenly deathless state
filled with sanctified grace.

I've been transported back to
when there was only nothing,
long before there was something;
and you and I were woven together
in a comfort of passion and peace,
transcending time, dimensions,
universes, realities and dreams:
All interchangeable.
And, all one in the same.

And though we are temporarily
parted in body and spirit,
for longer than an eternity,
soon I'll be with you again.

We will coalesce in spirit
and mutual reception
trading identities until
they are recognizable as only one.
A dual singularity,
and you and I will be we
forever connected to forever
bathing in the tears of love
and synaptic paths of tomorrow;
at last in the coveted climax
of redemption's salvation.

Sharing an alien algorithm,
beating in synch with blue stars,
we blend the ultrasonic waves
and the unstable lightning flashes
to match the rhythm we are,
infusing jazz music into our souls
with the needle of eloquent tones
as we travel the wind forest tunnel
of half notes and augmented chords.

Unfathomably cloaked in gauze
and unfashionably out of touch,
excommunicated strangers stand
in crooked attempts at attention
on the uneven road to the hereafter
that's littered with faded cut glass,
worn quartz and agate pebbles
ingrained in rough hewn stones.

I see a small shack on the roadside.
I enter in through the purple door
and see a large spacious emptiness.
An invisible band of retro-rockers
with broken instruments blares up
and the room races and reels
on a springboard dance floor
tailor-made for tip-top tap dancers.
They swirl and twirl in pantomime
parading by, holding their awards
high above their technicolor heads.
Holding them sky-high so the public
can't see the tarnished silver medals
cracked and crumbling,
dusted with windblown ashes
cloned from a dying star.

Rust painted and tainted robots
enter encompassing all things,
unfolding lackluster manifestations,
trying on realities and psyches,
bodies, flesh, bone and blood,
rags and remains of coveted wishes
and infinitely cherished memories.

Rusty painted, tainted robots.
Tin shells wanting to be humans.

Once again I am, far from this world,
away in a makeshift manger
      waiting to be:
a babe in arms seeking warmth,
a kung fu fighter in fields of war,
a mother longing for a long-lost son,
a father in training for natural suicide,
a fallen angel awaiting resurrection,
and a child of God ready to rise.

Once again I am waiting
to be reborn unto myself
forever and ever amen,

Journey

10 PAK — 2   Candice James

In the darkening shadows
of a fast-fading twilight
the sparkle of a summer star appear;
and far below, in Earthly robes,
a saintly figure stumbles by
chanting songs from long ago,
now buried deep in yesterday's ear.

There is a rhythm in the trees,
and the dampened feverish forehead
of a slowly recovering wind,
creeping through the grassy fields
alive in my mind's soft embrace
exemplifying the aroma of flowers,
at home in this ether I am.

I am a chunk of rarefied air,
bubbling in a sea of gasping water,
caught in a riptide of clashing clouds.

I move inter-dimensionally and
effortlessly into my other ether
to visit one of the other parts of me;
and my oversoul allows me to enter
in a push and pull fashion of static.

I am now looking through new eyes.
I am now walking through a new world.
I'm starting to blend into this other me.
I have no control over this entity.
I'm simply an undercover observer.

but still *...*
I feel every urge and every surge
and every itch and every pain.
For awhile I am this other me
but not able to influence, act or react.

but still *...*
I am aware of too many long nights
rocking a cradle of expired dreams
in the catch of an exhaled breath
trying to catch up with elusive death.

10 PAK — 2   Candice James

The shape of something unknown
is skulking on the shadow of a tear;
A tear that refuses to fall,
hanging on for dear life
in the land of the living dead,
alive for a moment then gone.

;
Blind in one eye,
and a patch on the other,
I can only see inside myself.

In the here and the now that is then,
I try to climb out of myself
and follow the dissolving footsteps
that led me to this place I am.

Time passes
        and passes
                and passes
           and then;

I'm riding on the wings of a falcon
invisible to everyone but me.
There's an eagle escort
with angels abride above
and an elegant blue heron
swooping the waves below.

In a hospital wing of another dream
I am waiting for a Dr. that never arrives;
and I will soon hold hands once again
with that dark invader I know so well.
My old friend and nemesis, death.

In the south of a northwestern sea
just below a frozen circle of dreams,
waiting to be reborn again and again
into the multiplicity of my forms,
I'm awaiting the calling of my number.

10 PAK — 2   Candice James

So I drift and I dream
inside my dream
that is dreaming of
the other dreams I am.

The ocean crests and runs free
like a child playing with a beach ball
and I am tossed as a lost feather
dropped from the wind-swept wing
of a low-flying wounded bird.

Can a dove enter into the yolk of an eye?
Can an Iris change color on a whim?
Can the hands of time ever turn back?
Can I ever find my reason for being?

10 PAK — 2   Candice James

There are fading chalk lines
on the sidewalk
where yesterday's hopscotch
once held court;
and there's a torn baseball
and a chipped, baseball bat
playing dead in a world
that's passed them by.

And the grass still grows and grows;
and the sky still cries and cries;
and the rain still falls and falls
in this tall grass wet world I travel.

I saw a red cloud bleed into blue sky
and I saw a universe shrivel and die.

    And then ...

I was drawn and quartered
       and shoved
into a deep, dark, pitch-black,
       black hole
and I became four separate entities
born again from out of my oversoul;
and we flew apart wingless
       and splintered
through the seven great divides
       of time
stacked on each other
     in timeless time
tangled in the tango of life
       and death
inside the gap between stillness
       and breath.

Melding with spirit
inside my oversoul
all my lifetimes appeared
in moving, majestic color:
The good, the bad,
the pretty, the ugly.

And all were accepted
as facets of learning.
Spokes in the wheels
of everlasting karma.
Lessons to polish each
stepping stone to a shine,
to perfect the spirit
to enter into the divine.

Then the air began to shake and pulsate.
I was a spark about to be born
from the womb of a black hole.
Living vibrant colors exploded
as thousands and millions of universes
were born and expelled
in the blink of an eye,

I stood outside time and myself
as faces and names
and moments flew by.

Some I cherished and loved
and some were sweet sighs;
but some were egregious errors
I had to relive and reset.

As the black hole closes behind me
I move through a tunnel toward the light.
I'm wet and I'm cold and uncomfortable.

I hear voices and see uniforms;
and beings I don't recognize.

I am shivering, frightened, and confused;
then I feel familiar arms encircling me.
I hear the voice I immediately recognize.
I fall to sleep in the arms of love.
In the arms of my mother once again.

>
> The journey is over
> and ...
> the journey begins.

10 PAK — 2   Candice James

In The Light

10 PAK — 2   Candice James

I walk through a field
of crimson and clover
where diamonds and gold
lie buried asunder.

The high snowy cliffs of Barritz Ombre
are melting beneath a hot siren sea.
I hear them softly calling to me
to fly on the wings of a wish
and come home to my oversoul
to be reborn again
to what I've always been born to be.

I walk into myself again and again
just missing my other self each time.

As I round the switchback bend
of sorrows and smiles
I feel hints of rain
swinging low in the mist
as I approach Dimension Seven.

Closer in,
the visions begin to appear,
twirling and swirling
around and above me.

They hold the lost films
of my hazy past
that fade in
               and out
of my being.

I stare in awe, but not in surprise.
I am them. I am each one of them
and all of them, each one is me.

Suddenly one of them breaks away
and latches onto my spirit.

The impact is powerful yet comforting.
The feeling is gentle yet passionate.
I become an ember in amber
slowly turning blue, red and purple
and then to evanescent white light.

I awaken totally from the dream of life.
inside a grand chamber of golden rods,
roses and lilacs of heavenly fragrance.

I'm escorted forward on a cushion of air
to stand ceremoniously
before a gleaming pink table
where a dozen luminous beings,
adorned in white robes and gold braid,
sit suspended on invisible seats
hovering in secrets and deep reflection.

Four small adult children surround me
and permeate my spirit
with love and glorious light;
and allow me to see myself
as I truly am.

I recognize my oversoul
floating toward me.

We rock and we roll
on an ocean of sweet tears
and glide through a cinematic
turquoise blue sky.

Then we come to rest
on a buffer of cloud
as we sink into the movie set
starring me and my *'selves'* ...

I am led through all the lives
I've lived well
then taken to the lives
I've wasted in sin.

I'm told I must relive
those wasted lives
and lay waste to the sins
I once embraced.

In a never-ending eternity
and the blink of an eye
I am transported back into
the Earthly realm.

Back into the life I am living now
fully aware of the sins I must assuage
to pay the price for my mistakes
so I can make this part of me
acceptable to blend into
and enhance the oversoul.

I close my eyes
and my soul comes undone.
I am the mist surrounding the sun.
I'm a snowflake
nestled in December's hand.
The wind blowing through
a golden hair strand.

With bluebirds on my shoulders
and a warm breeze at my back
I fly high above
sculpted white boulders
where crowds of clouds
stack and unstack.
in the midst of a murder
of jet-black crows.

A beautiful glowing ethereal freedom
washes over and cleanses my spirit.
In the distance I sense a soft melody,
at first very faint but now I can hear it.

It's a yawning and dawning
brand new day for me.

I am one. I am two. I am three.
I am every one of them
and they are all me.
I am the sky, the sand and the sea.
I am anything I choose to be.

For a double split second in time
like an extra word in a rhyme,
I'm a ghost in a pantomime,
refined and yet still undefined.

Behind the dark curtains
of a mahogany night
A star is born and is shining its light.
Inside this vacuum as black as coal
it's burning its beauty into my soul.-

I'm passing between
memories and dreams
where the memories are
a trove of lost dreams
and the dreams
are memories' children.

I am my father and my mother.
I am my sister and my brother.
I am me and I am not me
I am you and I am not you.

I am the nothing
that is everything
and the everything
that is nothing at all.

I am an anachronism unto myself.
A foggy night far, far from home.
A drop of sunlight lost in a wave.
A snippet of wind caught in a raindrop.
and a sharp-edged snowflake
    that burns like a poker
and scars the unsuspecting sky
      while its sleeping
    inside its own dream.

I am me, myself and I.
I am the earth, sea and sky.
I am spirit and life and death.

I am soul personified,
dignified and glorified
in the light of everlasting eternity
poured gently out
and filled graciously up
again and again and again.

10 PAK — 2   Candice James

10 PAK — 2   Candice James

Wings To Fly

10 PAK — 2   Candice James

Gliding through the kaleidoscope eyes
of a universe waking from a dream
angels and cherubs sit poised
at the gates of eternity
singing a hymn and a dirge
in simultaneous harmony and discord,
caressing and piercing
the ears of infinity.

    AND

I am walking in its wake
unperturbed by the sounds I hear.
Their whispers grow ever clearer
as they sidle up nearer
to this heart of hearts
that deigns to accept
the invitation of the wind.
and join in the song.

I lay down by the waters of Babylon.
I see a toy boat and water-wings
rocking and rolling gently
before the storms of life roll in:

To pluck at the unsuspecting soul
and scatter its essence to the wind.

To swoop up earth and harness air.

To form the beginnings
of new flesh and bone
and place the latent energy
in the pulsating womb of time
to await its next spirit sojourn.

The time spent in between breaths
is a time of intro and retrospection
infusing and readying the spirit
to rectify past errors and indiscretions
and help it plan, in detail,
how to repent and redeem itself
from the sins its gathered;
and how to cleanse the fields
it has sown bad seeds into.

The time for harvest will soon arrive
and the crop to be gathered will tell
the unedited and unredacted story
of how the spirit fared in its quest
to find sanctified redemption.

We are all children of God
born of the same genetic spirit.

We swim the ponds of childhood
and flail and flounder
at the whim of the wind.
A kind breeze or harsh hurricane.

The changes of soul temperature
are subject to the seasons as they pass
and the sensations we elicit from
souls we share the journey with.

We are the masters of our fate.
Sometimes the clowns of karma.
Sometimes the messengers
of good tidings or harsh woes.

But from inception to the end
we are all in this together
and yet separate unto ourselves.

We are a raindrop that cannot be split.
A snowflake that cannot dissolve.
A wind that cannot be destroyed;
A soul that's everlasting
and a spirit living in the catch
of eternity's never-ending breath.

The body is the land.
The soul is the sea.
The spirit is the sky
and redemption
gives us the wings to fly
forever free
in coveted eternity.

10 PAK – 2   Candice James

A Child Of God

10 PAK — 2   Candice James

I

When the wet night curls its inky fingers
around the stiff glass nape
of summer's blistered neck,
there is a shattering of unseen things
that speak in unintelligible languages.

Broken shells scratch and slide,
and tongue in cheek
squeak and speak,
as they drift across the sandy bottom
of a cold and discarded
second-hand ocean.

They can no longer
safely guide the moon
through the twists and hidden turns
on the seabed's seaweed
and kelp riddled highways
of the underwater sands.

One cannot anticipate
the angle of stars moving inside
the increasing and decreasing
progressive retrograde motions
of this spin-drift universe
riding on dusty, rusty wheels
through ancient planetary influences.

10 PAK — 2   Candice James

When moonlight falls in splinters
and the river makes no sound
as it passes behind the house,
there is silence of echoes
flowing through the sleeping trees;
their branches freeze stiffer than glass
at the wailing whispers
of the frost-bitten echoes
sliding and slicing above and below
and over and through
the mumbling, tumbling leaves.

How can one anticipate
the tone of dawn?
A sudden blaze of sunlight
cutting through the harsh sky?
A creeping ribbon of yellow silk
slowly scarfing the horizon?

Or simply ...
just a simple, slow breathing sunrise.

How can one forget summer evenings?

Hearts beating fast and fleeting
in the furious throes of new love.

Hands feverishly fumbling
to melt and blend flesh to flesh.

Souls tenderly touching
each other's eternity.

The impermanence
of all flesh and bone
eventually wrinkles
and splinters soundlessly
in the stone-cold recesses of the grave
or conversely ...
in the blistering inferno of fire.

All of which
is not spoken
of the spirit ... of the soul.

But here and now
in this little piece of life
behind drawn curtains,
gazing at the fire,
I think on how the earth spins dumb
and is bound by iron chains of frost
incarcerated in a broken piece of air;
and I imagine houses
on cold foggy streets
keeping the chill away
with windows tightly sealed
that still cannot keep death out.

And in these God-blessed houses
I envision orange cubes of firelight,
and antique Grandfather clocks
striking on the hour and quarter hour
with full Westminster chimes
echoing the hours of lost eras;
and I see families and friends
warming hands and hearts
in their circles of love and trust
waiting for winter to pass away.

As I walk the lonely streets of my life
I sometimes pass these houses
    and I ache
for the feelings they possess,
    for the close-kinit
      they are weaved in.

In the prime of my belated spring,
candles were small artificial suns:

> *Miniature flames*
> *swaying and flickering,*
> *constantly chasing*
> *the ice and snow away.*
>
> *Perpetual winters*
> *were totally unknown.*

Even when winter dared
to touch my cheek
I never doubted
the season's transience.

II

I have left the outside world ,,, outside.
I sit alone in my self-imposed exile.

I am far removed from people
and an unwelcome guest to emotions.

    I am a rock.
    I am an island
far removed from myself and my soul.

I am an outlaw riding the coat tails
of a runaway, renegade breeze.
A swift, unsure passenger
on a train bound for nowhere
seeking an undiscovered somewhere.
I'm drifting through dreams of strangers
strangled in the choke hold of lovers
    and ostracized
by family that is not familiar.

III

I have walked many beaches
and skipped many stones
on the oceans of tears
I unknowingly created.

I have sequestered agates
and semi-precious stones
in the frayed and ragged purse
attached to my weather-beaten wrist.

The stones and tears
wax continuously against each other
slowly destroying themselves.

Soon there will be nothing left.
No signs they ever existed.
No signs I ever existed

On this beach I find myself on today,
I lay myself down and close my eyes
to drift, drift and dream

Where am I?
Am I even real?
Or just a fading dream.

The heavy-laden vapor
of a long-lost night's sigh
is creeping and seeping into my eyes
and rearranging itself into tears.

10 PAK — 2   Candice James

I don't want to cry but the wet
is growing wetter and heavier
threatening to fill my eyes,
spill down my aging cheeks,
overflow the edge of my sorrow.
and drown any hope of tomorrow.

Sometimes inside these words
I think I'm at my end,
but then the end ends
and another unfinished beginning
hazes in and resumes.

IV

If I were a magician
with majestic powers
I would will the sun not to shine
and the moon and evening stars
not to come out of hiding.

And I would will the tides
to all be neap,
with no ebb or flow,
and the winds to be stiller
than death itself.

And when all these things
had come to pass
and the earth and universe
were at peaceful rest,
I would will myself
to float high above
and survey the stillness,
beauty and magnificence
of God's creation.

I would memorize every horizon.
I would harmonize every sound.
I would fly through every rainbow
into the arms of a breeze
born of a warm celestial wind.

I would listen to the stories
that would spill from its lips
in sighs and poems and songs;
and I would live inside them
    for a long while,
    for a short while,
for almost no time at all
but always aware of being
inside time never-ending.

If I were that magician
and I could choose to be
sun, moon, star, tides or wind,
I would choose to be the wind
so I could be gentle or wild
and touch all things living and dead
as I wandered the earth and skies
with a sweet benevolence overflowing.

I would contemplate God
living in every creature and creation.
I would purge myself
in the waterfall of purity and grace
that I may live in harmony
with God and Jesus and the angels
in His sanctified mansions in the sky,

I would endeavor to be
the true, pure, gentle child
He wants me to be
that I may live with Him
in grace and harmony
forever and ever ...
                Amen.

V

Oh yes, if I were a magician,
but, alas, I am not.

And oh ,,,
oh what a complicated entity
I am.

But always,
no matter what I am
or what I am not,
I am always,
always ...
a child of God.

Life And Death

10 PAK — 2   Candice James

I'm awake while I'm sleeping.
I'm hovering above myself
and at the same time
still within my flesh.

My eyes have grown heavy.
My body is frail and weak.
I can no longer feel the surge
of blood coursing through
my veins to warm my flesh.

I am disconnecting.
I'm alive but I'm dead.
I am solid but ethereal.
I am here and I am there.
I am inanimate and moving.
I am totally breathless
inside this limitless breath
in the entity of life and death.

10 PAK — 2   Candice James

I'm awake while I'm sleeping.
I'm hovering above myself
and now outside my flesh.

I am sliding on the dust of stars
and gliding on blue moonbeams.
I am the stardust.
I am the moonbeam.
I am everlasting
indestructible spirit.

Flying through the ether
of past, present and future
I arrive at eternity's door.

On the rising knowledge
of colour and tone
the steps are stacked like books.
I am a phantom standing
at the entrance to myself.

I climb the steps with expectation.
I move as mist, higher and higher,
toward the gate of heaven.

As I near I hear
a stir of wings and whispers.
Slowly the whispers dissipate
until there is only one voice.

Indistinct at first,
slowly growing louder,
I hear the echo of my name.
I feel the pull of an old
familiar magnetism.

You approach me with a rosebud
You kiss the flower; it opens.
You place it in my outstretched hand.

A flower grown in eternity's garden.
in full bloom at journey's end.

We come together as one
and lie in the palm of eternity'
at rest in a peaceful, easy feeling
of all encompassing colour and tone
and love's everlasting embrace.

I'm alive but I'm dead.
I am solid but ethereal.
I am here and I am there.
I am totally breathless
in this limitless breath.

I am alive
in the breath
of death.

Life is death.
Death is life.

Candice James is a writer, poet, visual artist, musician, singer/songwriter, and book reviewer. She completed her 2nd three-year term as Poet Laureate of The City of New Westminster, BC CANADA in June 2016 and was appointed Poet Laureate Emerita in November 2016.

She is Founder of: Royal City Literary Arts Society; Founder of The Fred Cogswell Award For Excellence In Poetry; Past President Federation of British Columbia Writers. Candice is a full member of the League of Canadian Poets, She has received Pandora's Collective Vancouver Citizenship Award; and the Bernie Legge Artist/Cultural award.

Her poetry has appeared in many international anthologies and her poems have been translated into Arabic, Italian, Bengali, Farsi and Chinese. Her artwork has appeared in Duende Magazine and in the "Spotlight" at Goddard College of Fine Arts, Vermont, USA and her poetry inside and artwork ("Unmasked") on the cover of Survision Magazine, Dublin, Ireland and her poetry and artwork have appeared in Wax Poetry Art Magazine Canada. She is the author of 28 books.

FOR MORE INFORMATION VISIT
website www.candicejames.com

www.ingramcontent.com/pod-product-compliance
Lightning Source LLC
Chambersburg PA
CBHW052142070526
44585CB00017B/1941